SALES AND MARKETING SUCCESS Blueprint

Written by Mike Leahy

This is a work of non-fiction. Written as guidance to anyone starting or having a small business who is looking for common-sense marketing ideas that are low-cost or no-cost. Ideas that have been tried and tested.

Copyright 2020 Mike Leahy
Published by Mike Leahy
Reprint 2021
Amended 2022

Please note: Edition License Notes

This book is licensed for your personal enjoyment only. This book may not be re-sold or given away to other people. If you would like to share this book with another person, please purchase an additional copy for each recipient. If you're reading this book and did not purchase it, or it was not purchased for your enjoyment only, then please return to your favorite retailer and purchase your own copy. Thank you for respecting the hard work of this author.

SALES & MARKETING SUCCESS BLUEPRINT

NOTE ABOUT 2020 ONWARDS

This book is re-written during the current crisis when so many people have lost their jobs or been on part-time wages or no income at all, when so many have lost money or used their savings, a disaster all round and no clear signs of when we may recover.

This book is brimming with marketing ideas that are free or cost little to implement but are tested and tried to be successful.

Whether you have an existing business or intend to start either a full-time business or a part-time business this small investment will help you to get off to a flying start.

There is a sister book that is over-flowing with ideas for creating a new business, 117 Small Business Ideas, that will help you decide on what you can best achieve.

I do hope that this book might help you towards a more secure future. Just remember all successful journeys start with one small step and then it is just a matter of putting one foot in front of the other. Sure, there are obstacles on the way which might take you back two steps but just keep looking towards the bright horizon and your future.

FORWARD ABOUT SOCIAL MEDIA

Some businesses have grown rapidly through social media and you can see these success stories every day, but I guess that for every successful business there are at least a thousand that have not reached such heights. So 1000 people decide to start their own business: 930 do nothing but day-dream about what they are going to do and how they are going to live a life of luxury (like the lottery, the number of high winners is small but most participants dream of what they would do if they won!), they have so many reasons for not starting. Of the 70 remaining probably 50 start writing a plan and five years later they are still trying to perfect that plan before they start; they never do!! Of the remaining 20, most do not have the dream or put in the effort; so probably just one business succeeds. The nine hundred and ninety-nine look at the success and think "That could be me" but if you don't do it now and take action, if you never finish the perfect plan, or if you don't put in the effort then zilch! Nothing.

And what are the biggest barriers? In my opinion they are firstly the fear of failure, Not being motivated enough, then by not taking action and finally by not being consistent. There are others "too old", "too young", "no experience", "no money", "next year I will" "not a good education", "too much happening in my life" and so on.

If you are younger than thirty years then you have been brought up in a total social media environment. Most social media platforms started after 2005, when Facebook was launched.

To anyone older the changes in communications have been unbelievable. And ways to sell have changed too. Before social media it was all person-to-person or advertising in newspapers and magazines or by leaflets. Sales-people spent all their time out with potential or repeat customers and spent little time in their office. Cold canvasing was common where you called at every building in a street or on an industrial estate looking for prospects, either business premises or people's homes, depending on the product or service. Now most offices are secure with a door entry system where access is becoming difficult. Now most canvassing for business is done by phone or social media including e-mail. The personal touch is disappearing, but is has not got altogether.

But I strongly believe that many of the old ways in combination with social media is the best opportunity for finding new prospects. This book outlines many of the original ideas and all have been proved as successful. So don't sit there thinking social media is the answer to your prayers, spread your wings, use every idea you can and then you have the best chance of success. Use a variety of marketing techniques, combine social media and direct selling. Some will fail so think about why they failed and either change them or lose them. Some will be successful, build on those.

Your marketing will change as you progress and you will make mistakes but as long as you are right more than 50% of the time then you are doing better than most of us. Mistakes are learning experiences, keep learning.

WELCOME

Welcome to this low-cost, no-cost marketing and sales book. It is straight forward, no-nonsense and direct so that you waste no time but can start improving your marketing immediately.

The ideas in this book are directed to local businesses but can be applied to online businesses too. Every idea has been tried and tested and each one will work and help you increase your sales. And all these apply whether you are starting a new business or want to build your existing business.

As with any business-related program, your results using Sales and Marketing Success Blueprint may vary from those of other businesses. Your own results depend on many variables, such as your determination and motivation, level of effort, business acumen, personal qualities, knowledge, skills, and other factors. Circumstances differ for everyone, and so we cannot guarantee, nor are we responsible for, your success, results, or income level. The Sales and Marketing Success Blueprint. is not a "get rich quick" approach. If making lots of money is your primary goal, this may not be the best option for you. We believe this program offers you the best tools for building your success as a business owner.

The aims of any business must primarily be to pay wages and salaries together with all overheads and to make a profit. That is the base and from there a business can grow, add branches, start franchising, and eventually be ready to sell. Build a business and then you have a choice: you can continue to build an empire or you can build until you have added enough value to sell the business and by selling you secure your future based on your previous efforts.

YOU CAN DO ANYTHING YOU WANT

Yes, it is true, provided you really want it and it's practically possible. You don't need a good education or be particularly clever. You don't need hundreds of contacts. You don't need bucket-loads of money. If you really want it, then you can achieve the impossible.

I worked with a salesman in London who was outstanding. He arrived at 7 o'clock every morning and was always with his first prospective customer at 9.00 if not earlier. We were selling telex and fax machines at around £2000 each. This was in the early eighties when that was expensive, fax machines dropped in price to less than £100 and now they are virtually redundant. This guy saw at least 5 prospects a day and was closing on average 10 deals a week. It was before mobile phones so he was using payphones when he was out and would be on the phone in the office from 8 o'clock. He was very direct and could make appointments within a few minutes. He had bought a large house, well above what an average salesman could afford and that was his motivation. He was the star salesman in the company. He kept going, not stopping for coffee breaks or other distractions. The concession he made was that he stopped working on Fridays at 4.30. His weekends were his own and he enjoyed them.

I met a young woman of 18 years who had started a domestic cleaning business. This was 15 years ago. She had £20 and couldn't even afford a vacuum cleaner. She used her customer's equipment. The £20 was spend on leaflets. She is now doing in excess of £4 million a year. I remember her telling me that she wanted to give the very best service at any cleaning company gave. She kept going and improving. At 21 years old she won the title "Young Entrepreneur of the Year" organized by the Federation of small business, beating over 1580 other entrants. Since then she has had a TV documentary about her, featured on many radio and TV shows and had several articles in national newspapers, magazines and been the subject of documentaries.

Personally, I have had my own successes. As a salesman winning trips to Amsterdam, Morocco, Toronto and New York, to name some. I had a paging business that was successful until mobile phones arrived that wiped me out. I got up again and started installing equipment for disabled people and gained large contracts with 7 local authorities including, Camden, Westminster, Brent, Hertfordshire and Harrow. Once I decided on my goal, I just went for it. I specialized in simple handrails, wooden ramps and door entry systems and then took on a carpenter, an electrician and a plumber to undertake other work. I rented a workshop and started cleaning and refurbishing disability equipment for local authorities as an extension to the business, employing two people. Then I formed a company and we manufactured tactile signed for businesses (used by visually impaired people as they had raised text and images).

And you can do the same.

You need to be focused. You may be without a job, owe money big time, live in a tiny flat. You can turn yourself around and be a winner. When I say focused, I mean really focused. You will live your dream and forgo other interests at least until you are seeing success, and even then, ***you must keep going***. When a friend says, "come on, let's go out for the evening", you've got to say "NO!" When you feel tired or things are not going well, you must keep going. You never know how close you are to success. You must become an eternal optimist.

Know When to Stop.

On the other hand, you need to judge the time to stop a project if it isn't working for you. You aren't going to be right first time, every time. And in fact, if you are right more than 50% of the time, then you are doing better than the average person.

SALES & MARKETING SUCCESS BLUEPRINT

The average number of business started by entrepreneurs before they found success is over 15 businesses. That's right. Even the most successful have had a mountain of failures. You often only hear about the successes. It's not unusual for showbiz overnight successes have been trying to win for 25 years or more. Suddenly they are in the limelight and seem to have had overnight success. And this seems to be a problem. Many young people want instant success: they see YouTube influencers, sports-people and winners on X-Factor and fail to know about the training athletes and other sports-people endure, sometimes 6 or 7 hours a day of punishing physical workouts, even the YouTube influencer may have worked solidly for a few years to get it right and build a following. There is no gain without pain . . . but you can do it!!

So, when you start a new project do your very best, carry out all the steps needed to be successful and keep records. Don't give up at the first hurdle, persevere and if it's not working after a reasonable time then STOP. Take stock of the things you did right and those you did wrong. Now continue with that project or find your next and do the things that worked but forget the rest for now. They may work in the new idea, but you must concentrate on the successes first. *Never give up!* You might stop one project and start another but never give up on your dream of being successful. With determination it will happen.

Surround Yourself with Positive Successful People

This will instill success and keep you positive and motivated.

Have you ever sat with miserable negative people? Constantly complaining, sharing their problems and always seeing the worse? How did that make you feel? Now think of a time when you were with a group of positive people and compare the difference in how you felt. Attitude is so important.

In general, positive people take risks, take actions and, when things go wrong (as they do for all of us from time to time) they can shrug it off and find a solution. And that is what you want to do every time.

It reminds me of the story of the two shoe salesmen who were send to an African country. It was hot and the people living there lived simple lives, none wore shoes.

The only lane through the village was sandy, no sharp stones.

The first salesman messaged back *"I'm returning home. Nobody wants shoes here"*

The other salesman wrote "*Great news, nobody is wearing shoes yet, a great opportunity*"
Which would you be??

Make Time to Think!

It is essential that you give yourself time to work on your business, and not spend all your time working in your business. Remember this is a business and not a job. A business is created to grow, to employ more people and pay their wages and all expenses, make more profit over and above the running cost to build a future. A job might be where you work for yourself but just want to continue as you are, alone, and bringing in enough for you to live. That is not a business. You may as well work for somebody else and not have the worries associated with a business.

So, you need to put some time aside every day to look at how your business is working, who your customers are and will be, changes that will improve the business. I clearly remember visiting a small business, employing about half a dozen people. They had a production plant producing personalized products. The boss was out on the floor all morning working with the team producing the finished work for delivery or installation in the afternoon.

He stopped when I arrived and we went to his office as we were going to discuss some simple marketing for him to work on. The phone rang a couple of times and he interrupted our meeting to answer: the production guys called him for instructions or to look at a finished job and he went out to the floor. Our meeting was scheduled for an hour. He spent less than 30 minutes with me. Now I was paid for the appointment time, so it didn't matter to me, but I did corner him as we drew to a conclusion. I shut the door, took the phone off its cradle and sat back. "What the hell are you doing!" he shouted.

"Calm down a minute" I said. "We had a meeting scheduled for an hour and it was cut short every few minutes. I don't think you've had the concentration to remember what we discussed" He looked at me.

"Well we are busy; I'm trying to run a business here"

"I understand that" I replied "But listen . . . "and I went on to suggest to him to slow down, delegate and spend more time managing. It was a month before I saw him again. He took me into the office, got one of the lads to make us coffee and shut the door.

I was dubious about what he would say after our last meeting, but I needn't have worried. "Mike, I didn't realize how crazy I was working until you told me last month. I've got work schedules laid out each night for the following day, my brother checks each job. I don't think I trusted him fully before, young brother and all that. And I've got an answering service, so I switch to them if we are really busy or if I'm in my office planning." I looked at him "Yes. You were right. I spend about 30 minutes each morning in here, door closed and no interruptions. I thought everything was urgent but realize that everything can wait half an hour!"

I was very relieved. About a year later at a meeting he said "Mike, that was the best advice I've ever had. It helped me grow this business dramatically, thanks"

PILLARS TO BUSINESS SUCCESS

So, first here are the three pillars of any business. They are all equally important and if one is weak then the effect will be felt throughout the business.

Product or Service

I know it's obvious, but you must have a product or service that people either need or desire, that is available to sell and does what it says at a price that customers will pay.

Some products are needed such as basic groceries, but many are desired such as a new car when the existing one will do the job. The product must be available to sell, but that may mean that it will be available at an acceptable future date. If you want a new kitchen fitted you may have to wait for a fitting team to be available for example. The product must do what you claim of it to satisfy the customer and trading standards. It must be at a price the customer will pay, this is relative and means different things to different people, a millionaire might be able to afford a helicopter, a factory or office worker might be able to afford a newer car. But although they might not be able to afford to pay cash there are always alternatives such as credit cards, loans and rentals.

Finance

You must have the capital to buy in the products or components to manufacture them before you can sell them. If you have no capital or ways to raise capital then in most cases you are sunk before you start. There are exceptions for example the entrepreneur starting a gardening service might just need a few tools and away he goes, getting paid each day at the end of the job he is undertaking. Then as he gains more business and profit that he can plough back into the business he can buy more equipment, a vehicle, premises and invest in staff. In every business you need employees, and every employee will help the business grow still further.

But that is just half the story. The most important elements in finance are getting paid and making a profit.

Sales & Marketing

You must be able to find people and persuade them to pay for the goods and keep them. Find the people is the marketing element and there are many ways to seek out customers. Persuading them to give you money in exchange for the goods is the selling aspect. And getting customers that return over again will help reduce your marketing and sales costs. We'll cover both marketing and sales here..

Profit is King

You should not be trying to just increase turnover. You goal is to keep increasing your profit. There is a saying "Turnover is vanity, Profit is sanity"

And here's why!

Your turnover (the amount of money you receive for sales) must cover all your overheads and that includes:

Cost of the Products you buy, or the components you need to carry out the conversion to the product or service you sell.

Staff wages/salaries that you pay out weekly or monthly.

Utilities such as electricity, gas, telephone and internet

Rent for the premises

Vehicle purchase or rental.

Fuel, road tax, maintenance for that vehicle

Incidentals such as postage, meals you must buy when working, small equipment etc.

Capital Equipment, the equipment you buy or rent to use in your business

Your salary or dividend you pay yourself

(This list is not exhausted, this is just an indication) This turnover must be enough to cover your costs. It might just break even, or it might give you some left over which is the profit. As the business grows the turnover will grow but so will the cost of everything.

Your profit is what is left over after the costs are deducted. So, this is the key factor that you need to grow to be successful.

So, you see that PROFIT IS KING. It is the very heart of the business and if you make no profit, then you have no business. Often there is no profit for the first few weeks or months but as a small business you must not allow that to continue by borrowing unless you are guaranteed future success. So many businesses crash, and the owner is often left with debt. The aim here is to give you plenty of ammunition to fire at the target (prospective customer) so you can capture them, and they place an order.

So, remember to keep your eye on the profits.

INCREASING PROFITS

This is the primary aim of any business - to make a profit. If you are just taking a wage and not extra profit, then it is just a job, and you might as well work for someone else.

Roads to Profit

There are few routes to increasing profits. Basically, it breaks down to the following.

One. Get more customers. If you are selling a product that is going to last for ever then you need to keep finding new customers. If your customers keep returning then you will need some new customers to replace the ones you lose. Every business loses some customers for a variety of reasons. A customer may think he will get a better deal from a competitor: He might have a friend who can supply him: he might cease trading, retire or even die, he might not personally like you. These are some legitimate reasons you will lose customers and you can do little to stop them going. Just make sure you do not lose customers because you fail them, fail to deliver on time, you do not give good service, or you are rude to the customer (we hope not but it does happen!!)

In addition to this turnover and replacement of customers you need to find more. These extra customers will bring in extra profit. Think about this: your existing customers pay all your overheads and your wages. Addition customer's profit on sale is all net profit, they don't have to contribute to your overheads or wages.

Two. Sell more to existing customers. You may need to find additional products or services that you can offer. Remember, existing customers like and trust you so that selling them additional products will be easier than selling to new prospects and will be quicker to produce orders.

Three. Reduce your overheads. You should always be looking to cut your overheads without reducing the service. Look for legitimate cuts, better prices from a supplier, your staff doing more. Even small savings can help. Signs on light switches "Switch off when not in use" were popular during national strikes in the eighties and did save money. But do not reduce the quality you offer by buying in poor quality components or products you are going to re-sell.

Four. Increase your prices. This is the other way to increase profits but the riskiest. You might lose enough customers that the increase in price doesn't bring in more revenue!!

Summary.

So those are the basic ways to increase profits. Work on these principals and succeed. You can use all those ideas: more customers, sell more to existing customers, cut your overheads, increase prices. Think about it. If you could increase profits by just 2.5% in each area then your profits would increase in total by 10%.

CASH FLOW STARTS HERE

You need a process in place to make sure you get paid. Sounds something you'd do anyway. Well! Many business slip up here and either don't get paid at all, or find that they are chasing for the money, or that the buyer (mainly large businesses don't pay for 60 or 90 days) and that will be a problem because you will have your overheads and costs, you will have the sale money due to cover those costs and if there is a hold up what will you do?

Set out conditions when you sign off the order
Always invoice on the day you deliver or before if possible. I've known businesses wait until the end of the week before invoicing the customer which then adds time before you get paid. ALWAYS invoice on the day.

Terms - tell before you sell - and get agreement. It's a good idea to have terms and conditions on the reverse of the order form. Get the customer to sign an order or, if online, have a tick box where they agree to your terms.

Think about payment in advance, stage payments, payment due 14 days instead of 30. Discount for immediate payment. I've even got local authorities to pay up front which is almost unheard of. You must be strong and ensure you can deliver on time to the agreed quality. If you aren't upfront with this, then you may have disappointing delays in payments.

Statements to arrive 3 days before due date. Phone on the due date and follow up any action such as calling within a week if money hasn't arrived. Oh, and put an advert on all invoices and statements about special offers, quantity discounts, repeat orders etc. Never miss a chance to advertise to existing customers.

Ordering Dept Ensure you can get products, you can supply satisfactory quality, you can deliver on the promised date, you have someone who will personally take care of this (as a one-man show that will probably be you!).

WORKING PLAN

You must have a plan of what you want to achieve and how you'll get there. Imagine setting out on a long car journey without a plan, a map showing you the route, what you want to achieve: maybe how long the journey will take, what time you will arrive and if you might stop for a break. You might also take food and drink for the journey.

Same with your business, you must have a plan. This doesn't have to be an involved 20-page comprehensive plan that you write and then put in a draw in your desk and never look at again. You need an Action Plan that you look at frequently and that you can adjust according to your progress, and challenges along the way, or any good fortune that will increase your profits.

I recommend you keep a loose-leaf folder and check it out at least every other day. This will make more sense as we progress through this book.

The old saying absolutely applies "Plan your work and work your plan."

ACTION

Get yourself an A4 loose leaf ring binder. This will grow to be full of ideas to increase profit in your business. Write in, refer to and keep this Folder to the front every day.

Your action folder should include these ideas and you should look at them after a few days to see if they a practical. If they are then do a test.

Your action folder should include your forthcoming activities as bullet points that you can strike out as you complete them. And add new activities. This way you keep on top.

THE RULES OF MARKETING

There are no rules except be regular and consistent and if something doesn't work then move on to something else.

If there were rigid rules of marketing, then every business would be doing the same thing. Some say marketing is a science, others say it's an art. I'd go between. But the only rule I would say is test, test, test and compare the results. You can write two identical sales e-mails with just a couple of words changed and find dramatic differences in the results.

Act by trying a marketing tool like a leaflet, advert on social media, having signs on your vehicle. Do it today. And you can design your own leaflets, adverts and business cards using www.canva.com, which have a free section. This site is a must. If you are rubbish at design get a friend to help until you can afford a professional designer. For print in the UK I use www.solopress.com

Monitor the results. Ask people if they have seen your marketing and what do they think. Keep asking questions. By the way if you ask family and friends, they will normally be positive. Ask strangers and more often they will be honest and will tell you what is right or wrong. What they like or hate.

Then make changes. And continue doing this with all your marketing and you will begin to see more interest.

REMEMBER!

If you win more than 50% of the time you are ahead of the game and better than the majority. If you do it and get it right more than 75% of the time you will have outstanding success. Mistakes are a learning experience so don't be afraid to make them, the fear of failure stops most from progressing. Try, try and try again.

LEARN FROM OTHERS

But remember that learning from other people's mistakes is better than learning from your oqn. So, watch what other businesses do, look at your successful competitors and learn from them. Look at adverts, vehicle signage, leaflets, social media, their premises, business cards.

It is cheaper to learn from others. In fact, it's – FREE. If you must learn from your mistakes you will have to pay for printing costs and your time.

It is faster to learn from others. It is quicker because you don't have to go through the experience

It makes you look cleverer than you might be.

Get the basics right and that's what we are going to concentrate on today.

WORKSHEET
STEPS TO TAKE NOW

You are now keeping an action and marketing plan loose leaf folder. Here is the next sheet to complete and add in.

Think about your own business and write down the ideas that are covered in this book that you could use.

Do you know who your ideal customer is?
Describe that customer How can you contact them as a group? E-mail? Blog? YouTube? Social media such as Facebook, Instagram or Twitter.

Write down a selection of marketing ideas and then mark off the effectiveness, cost and effort in using each one. Remember that a good marketing idea should be able to reach those people easily and in a targeted fashion: low-cost in relation to the return you'll make it should be simple to implement.

Importance of Keeping Records. . . . . . and reviewing them. Records show the way forward by looking at the past. We can see ideas that work and those that don't. Then we can go forward, look at the failures and learn from them. Look at the successes and build on them. Much of this is already available on social media.

Record Details of Prospects. Yes, you can do that on your laptop, but I use physical 5x3 cards and write on them. And keep them in a box visible when I'm working. They are in alphabetical order and divided into how soon I feel they will develop into an order. Keep details of the name. contact name, phone numbers, e-mail and personal information you have picked up (such as their children, hobbies, holidays and so on) On the reverse keep details of your contact with them, phone calls, discussions about orders and actual orders if they are a regular customer, if you meet them, and what is discussed so you can continue on next time you speak, fully reminded.

I have three sections in 5x3 record box, the front is customers who should order very soon or are regulars, the second section is those who might order in the next month that you have spoken to, the last section is the rest who you need to keep in contact with.

Keep a diary. Write down your appointments, physical and phone, orders, future dates when you promise to do something. You can do this on your phone. Then you have it with you always. This can be a diary on your phone but I personally also keep a A5 diary, personal choice.

Although we are in the digital age and your phone has a calendar think about keeping a paper diary. A notebook with lined paper is adequate. Write down everything. Successes, failures, how you have achieved things, names of contacts, ideas to increase the business. This will be invaluable as your business develops.

SALES & MARKETING SUCCESS BLUEPRINT

WORKSHEET

Sit Down on Your Own with a Notepad and Work Out these figures in Your Office

1. Have you a record of your turnover and profit for the last 12 months?

2. What was the turnover? £

3. What was the net profit for the last 12 months? What you are left with when you have taken out all your costs and earnings? £

4. What is the average price of your individual products £

5. What is the average net profit on your individual product £

6. How much did you spend last year on advertising and other marketing £ (Yellow pages, newspapers, magazines,

7. What was your ROI (return on Investment) for the last 12 months £ (Net profit (3 above) against Advertising Spend (6 above)

Do you consider this is high, average or low?

Do you feel you should spend less to achieve more?

How can you work smarter not harder?
You must become aware of your success rate and the best way is to check out your past results. Then you can set realistic targets and compare actual on-going results against the past the targets you set. Targets must be realistic, and you should set a reward for achieving, whether for staff or yourself

Business Cards, Stationery, Website, Vehicle

You will be surprised how many businesses leave off critical information on their day-to-day stationery, websites and vehicles. And that information should be fast and easy to read.

I'm talking about these basics.

Landline and Mobile phone numbers. Look on the internet, you can get very low-cost "free to ring" numbers where you pay a small fee for every call you receive. Everyone likes the word "FREE" and freephone, even when most people now have a call bundle where they only pay extra if the reach their plan limit. You can divert your home or office landline to your mobile and never miss a call. Or you can sign-up to an answering service where you pay a monthly fee or a cost per call, or a combination of both. Few people like answer machines or having to leave a message. Nobody likes waiting for a call be answered or having to leave a message so whenever possible try and answer within two rings. Obviously this isn't always possible but do your best.

The Address. You may not want to broadcast your home address on your vehicle, but you can put a town or district so that people know you are local. Once again, there are businesses that will take in your mail and forward it on or hold it awaiting you to pick it up.

Website. Include your website on everything. Its now common to cut out the *www*. As this is standard. Cutting it out makes the website easier to remember and see.

e-mail. I am constantly surprised at the e-mail addresses used. Often, they are personal. Far better to link your e-mail to your website. So if your website is www.acmecleaning.com then you should be able to have orders@acmecleaning.com, info@acmecleaning.com and so on. You just need to look at your domain name detail and usually you can set this up yourself under e-mail. Then, if you wish you can direct that to your personal e-mail, so when one is sent to the business it is forwarded to you. I have several e-mail addresses all directed to a single e-mail and I can see each one instantly, anytime, at the click of one button.

Incidentally, it is both good business and a common courtesy to reply to all e-mails within a reasonable time, I'd propose within 2 hours. Even if you reply that you've received the e-mail and will send a full reply within 24 hours, or whatever your policy is.

Tagline You should have a tagline that you use everywhere that describes your service. "Fast Friendly Service", "Never beaten on customer service", "Free quotation. No Obligation". These are some general taglines. People will associate that with you, but you must follow up and meet the promise, every time.

BUSINESS CARDS IN PARTICULAR

Call for Action Always have a call for action, "call this number", "do it now!", go to the website". This does work and encourages people to do what you write.

The Reverse Is there anything on the back of your business card. You can use this for appointment details, advertising, more details about your business for example. I once worked for a company that provided 150 business cards each month: every month there was an advert for a different product. Part of our job was to give them out each day. I used to leave them on bus seats, in library books, in shops and other public places, plus I would give them away to potential customers and at meetings. It was quite successful. Each advert had a code so we could track who had given the card out and which month.

Clear for writing notes Try to leave some white space. You'd be surprised how often you want to make a note on a card, usually only a couple of words. Could be a simple "Thanks" or a time. Could be a product code.

Guarantee You should include a guarantee line where you offer one. "12 months free guarantee on all our products" Always try to use the word "free" where you can. It has great pulling power.

Handy hints You might put a handy hint on the product, it could even just be a general hint or "How to". We all love hints and tips.

STATIONERY

We are so dependent on e-mails now that many businesses never use their own stationery. Sometimes it pays to send letters and invoices by post or drop them off. Customers leave correspondence on their desk so its like a constant reminder of you. In addition, you can incorporate and advert into an invoice (you should do this with electronic invoices too). We are so accustomed to marketing e-mails that it is often refreshing to receive a sales letter.

WEBSITES

Always put contact details at the top of each page. Not everyone wants to e-mail you, give them the opportunity to phone you. On some websites it is almost impossible to find a phone number, and this is most frustrating. OK! Often, you'll get a customer with a complaint. You should look at that as a good thing. If they don't call to complain then likely they will tell all their friends what a lousy

company, you are. If you get a complain follow the three-point plan.
1. Apologize and put it right.
2. Find out what went wrong
3. Make sure it doesn't go wrong again

Address. Always include your business address, when people see a box number, they get suspicious.

Directors or Owners. Not many businesses show the directors, but they should be listed. This complies with the law, but also it shows you are a real business with real people who will make decisions. You also need to show your company registration number.

Easy Navigation. The average time a surfer stays on your website when he lands first time is less than 3 seconds, so it needs to look interesting, simple and easy to navigate. Many sites are just one page now with the different sections running down the page. Still many businesses do not have a website. Build your own. It's easy and if you use Wix.com it can be free if you don't mind a small advert. If you want a shop, then you'll have to pay. Wix is easy to use and you can adapt one of their many templates or design your own. I've had free and paid Wix sites and I forward my domain name to the Wix site, so it is personalized. You might have a big presence on social media, but a website is a very useful marketing tool that you should have.

Up to date. Make sure your website is current. I've seen several recently with out-of-date details including opening hours, phone numbers and product details. It doesn't take but a glance each week to check your website out.

Testimonials are such a good marketing tool. Persuade some customers to write a review and try to get their photo too. Testimonials can be the strongest attraction for potential customers. You may write glowing information about your products or services, but viewers will more believe what other people (testimonials) write.

Guarantees put customer's minds at rest. Money back guarantees are a winner. You may feel that customers will take advantage and return goods unnecessarily, especial digital products that they can download then want a refund. You'll get some but the benefits of many extra customers outweigh this.

Call to Action is the positive way to get prospective customers to buy. "Call this number now", "just fill in your name and e-mail and we'll send you . . .", "We are only a phone call away, pick up the phone now". These calls to action are very powerful.

Free reports are a magnet. Offer a Free Report and the responses will give you names and e-mail addresses that you can use to follow up. Make you report useful and full of information. You will need an e-mail service. Mailchimp.com has a free entry level which will satisfy most small businesses. This works complimentary to your website and is essential.

Free reports do not need to be long, technical or comprehensive. They may cover one aspect of the solution you are selling, data or general facts, a how-to report, or anything of interest about your products, services or your company.

YOUR STAFF

In this book I include not only those who work for you directly but anyone who is a contractor or does part-time work. **These are you biggest asset.**

Look after them.

Train them. You must train your staff in all aspects of your business. They not only need to know everything about the products or services but how you handle the phone, complaints, orders.

You should always listen to them. You'll often find out improvements, new ideas and overcoming problems by listening. This does two things: it solves a problem and it tells your staff you appreciate them. I once worked for an international company, huge. I worked in sales in the Head Office at Euston, London and there was a staff restaurant (in 1968 there were waitresses! No queuing). If we arrived before 8am we had free coffee and a very cheap breakfast, and this encouraged us to arrive early and start the day with a light meal. One of the two directors was always there early and would sit and talk to the staff. If you gave them an idea that they used, then they rewarded you with a gift. Sometimes it was a meal out for two, other times it was money. This was a good incentive for some of the staff.

You should take an interest in your staff and remember details about them. There is nothing that produces loyalty more than the boss asking specifically about a member of your family, your hobby, sport or something similar.

Praise costs nothing but reaps rewards. We all love genuine praise and if you can find something to praise an employee about, that will make their day.

I remember working for the same company in London and was ill with pneumonia. The directors sent a basket of fruit and chocolates, delivered by their chauffeur. That is the ultimate in staff care.

If you have managers or team leaders encourage them to look after their people well.

Incentives for Staff are important. And they do not have to be expensive. It depends on the additional benefits your staff will bring. I have personally been to New York, Toronto, Amsterdam, Cannes and had a weekend in a good hotel in London with all expenses paid, including a chauffeur car show and nightclub. I've been to top sports events and

Your staff are your most prized asset provided you look after them. Wages/salary is important but personal interactions are equally important.

TELEPHONE ANSWERING.

We all get annoyed when the phone isn't answered or we are put on hold and wait. A good policy is to try to answer the phone within 2 rings. We've all seen the phone ring in a shop and the staff keep chatting to each other!! Make them aware of your expectations.

They should answer in the name of the business not "Hello!". Simply say "Good morning/afternoon xxxx business how can I help you?" Saying Good morning or afternoon alerts them to your voice, so they hear the name of the business when you continue. "How can I help you" encourages them to tell you what they want? After they have told you, then repeat back so there is no confusion.

Always try to be explicit, try to give accurate prices, delivery dates, start times and so on.

COMPLAINTS

We all hope we get no complaints and you should be trying to supply the best products or services on time at a competitive price (not the cheapest!!) so there should be few complaints, but things do go wrong.

When you get a complaint in person or on the phone then
- listen carefully,
- ask the name of the person,
- repeat in your own words what they say the problems is,

- ask them what they would like you to do about it, and do just that, if it falls within the business policy. That might be repair, replace with a new product or offer a refund. Nobody likes refunding but sometimes it is sensible and reduces further costs or time wastage.

These are the three steps when a customer makes a complaint:
- Put it right
- Find out what happened and why it went wrong.
- Ensure it doesn't happen again.

The Customer is King! The customer is always right! This used to be the mantra, but we all know that isn't true. However, **the customer always deserves respect**, even when you must tell them they are wrong! Just remember.

GET YOURSELF SEEN

Try the following ideas. All of these are proven ways to be seen and bring in more prospective customers.

EXHIBITIONS

Exhibitions are a good way to be seen. Business-to-business exhibitions have been running for years and are still a low-cost way to meet many potential customers. They are held locally and nationally. Unless you have a large budget, you need to concentrate on local exhibitions, but here is a tip I've used several times to rustle in on national exhibitions at a low price, and once even for free.

I would follow the build up to exhibitions and see how the uptake was going. On the day before the show opened, I'd call the organizers and see if there was any low-cost or free space available. I've been lucky on about half of the exhibitions I've attempted this with. So, it's a gamble but if it pays off, you'll get a stand for peanuts. If you lose, so what, you knew the chances. If the stands are being booked fast and early then this technique will not work. Then you need to book your space before all stands are taken.

I've run local exhibitions and been successful. I would pitch the stand price to be as fair as possible but also to give me a reasonable profit. As an organizer there is the cost of the venue, flyers and posters, together with other materials such as tickets, staff to man the event, newspaper and local tv advertising (although it's better to get some interviews and get free coverage). You've also got to work to fill all spaces. If it works you might expand. In my location, one Show Organizer has been running successful shows for about 8 years and has grown to hold them in about three other locations. It has turned into a full-time business.

As an exhibitor it is generally not possible to pack up the car and pop along, quickly set up your stand and start selling, you need to plan in advance and often arrive the previous day to set up. Here are some of the steps you should take.

Book the Stand. You can jump in early and try to get a stand near the food area or entrance. At the entrance you'll be seen first and that can be positive. Be near the food or bar and visitors will linger and see you for longer than when they walk around.

Invite Customers. You should invite both existing potential customers. That way you'll keep in touch with existing customers, be able to chat with them in a semi-sales atmosphere and show them new products. You can test the water and may pick up some orders but in addition you will be able to follow up. You should build up a good relationship with existing customers and an exhibition is a good stepping stone. Obviously prospective customers are invited so they can see, touch and possibly use the product and you should be looking to getting an order signed, probably with a special exhibition offer or discount. Some exhibitors are afraid of inviting customers for fear of losing them to a competitor. If your product is good, your service the best you can give and the price competitive you should have no fears. And be a good listener. **Good salesmen don't have the gift of the gab but listen properly and find solutions.**

Train your Staff. So important. Show them the basics that you require, cheerful, polite, smartly dressed and friendly. If they are wearing a suit, then the tie should be up tight. They should all wea a name badge. It must be easy to read so use a plain typeface. Concentrating on the person they are talking to, not using their mobile at any time on the stand (not even to look at), knowledge of the products or service you are offering, and discounts they can offer, and very importantly to make a record of everyone they talk to so you can follow through after the show. You need name, e-mail, business name, phone number, address and a few details of their interest. Collect this information throughout the day and keep it safe (I've known competitors stealing lead forms that have been left on a desk)

Breaks. Make sure the stand is manned throughout the day so stagger breaks. If the staff leave the stand tell them to keep their mobile phones switched on in case, you need them back. Breaks are important to keep everyone alert.

The Stand. Be on site early and check the stand is as you ordered, clean and the power is working. There is usually an electrician on hand to fit extra lights or replace faulty bulbs. Check the signage. Check the products are shining clean and work properly (If applicable). Make sure you have your literature ready, leaflets, brochures and each staff member has business cards. Flyers and business cards are dirt cheap online so order enough.

You may need a desk. I'd recommend a small standing desk. There is nothing worse than seeing someone sitting behind a desk, alone, probably using their mobile phone!! A standing desk means you can take down information from a new customer giving you an order but standing up will make you more alert and you can move on faster. If the visitor is sitting down, they are more likely to stay longer. A chair or two is ok, provided there is space and that you or your staff don't sit relaxing there. You need to be on your feet, greeting.

Stands should be bright, screen displays of your products, coloured lights and any movement that attracts the eye will encourage visitors to take a second look. Make sure everything is clean and sparkling both on the walls and furniture. Clear away rubbish constantly.

Don't stay at the back of the stand. The edge is like a physical barrier and many people won't cross that line. Stand near the edge of the stand and smile. Outstretch you hand with a leaflet, brochure or product. When a visitor reaches out step back, smiling and they will step forward too. "I'm Mike. Are you enjoying the show? What are you most interested in today?" don't be pushy. Let them speak and you can tell roughly whether they are a prospective customer or not. But never judge. Some visitors are professional buyers and have a poker face, some have come in the middle of a busy day and in working clothes. You can't tell by the way people appear.

Welcome existing customers and show them new products, be relaxed. This is an occasion with them that is quite informal. You might get an order, especially if you can offer something special, the exhibition price or free attachment for example.

Take time to go around the show and look at your competitors. Are they doing something that you are not? Look at other stands for ideas. Watch how other salespeople work. Give your staff the opportunity to go around the show too.

Keep the records safe. Collect names, emails, phone numbers etc. and keep these safe. When I was a young salesman, I remember the manager made us fill up a book with all the visitor details. Towards the end of the first day, the book disappeared. We think a competitor picked it up. It was a great loss to our Company.

PRIVATE EXHIBITIONS

Selling office equipment and other business equipment or services, home products or services? Holding a private exhibition/show is a great way to get your business known and to make extra sales.

Hire a room in a hotel, community centre or shopping centre. Advertise well and promote with adverts in local papers, social media, phoning potential customers, calling existing customers and even getting some posters printed and see if local shops will display then for 2/3 days, such a short time might be acceptable. One exhibition I was organizing I stood at the side of the road dressed as a penguin holding a massive poster at rush hour times where the traffic was running slow. It worked.

I remember a photocopier company that held a holiday exhibition every year when they would set up as a holiday destination in their showrooms to promote their products. One year it was Paris with waiters with long black aprons, berets and moustaches, an accordion player. They served French bread with cheeses and other French savories. It didn't cost much but was very successful together with a glass or red or white wine. Every year their existing customers looked forward to the event and wondered what country would be represented next. The Company always send out picture postcards as invites saying, "Wish you were here" and the picture was of the country.

There are many ideas you can implement.

I had a business who set up in the local shopping centre, they made it bright and welcomed people in for a small cake and a candy bar for the kids. This was successful. The Shopping centre welcomed them and didn't charge them. You might have to negotiate. Try and get someone interesting like a juggler, magician or clown to be on the stand.

Working with a photocopier company I remember we held a private exhibition every two months in a different location. We'd try and do a deal with the owners, so we had a low-cost or free space, usually in return for some copying. If you are bringing along a limited number of visitors, then offer to collect them and return them after. Transporting visitors is a positive way to ensure they arrive. Too often people promise but never turn up. You should call them the previous day to remind them and even on the exhibition day "Hi . . . . I am looking forward to seeing you later to show you our new product. You said you'd be here around 11.30?"

LEAFLET/FLYER DROPS

Flyers cost peanuts today. A5 is most popular, half a letter size. And maximize by using both sides in full colour. Use www.canva.com to create the artwork or look online at some printing companies who produce leaflets and they may have templates to make life easy for you.

Short of money and time? Get another business that doesn't conflict with you to advertise on the reverse side. So, if you are a plumber, maybe an electrician would be interested in working with you. Work out distribution and do half each. Don't expect to distribute 5000 leaflets in a day. It just isn't possible.

The best plan is to do a street or two (no more than 200 letterboxes during the day). Then call back in the evening, knock and introduce yourself. Don't waste time. Just say you left a leaflet, you are a (your job) and ask if they have any work for you or know anyone who might. Don't push. By calling

SALES & MARKETING SUCCESS BLUEPRINT

back you make your chances of success so much better: They see you face-to-face and people do make snap judgements on appearances so look smart and clean. A gardener doing this increased his success from 1 in over 500 to 1 in every 50 homes he called on. Not bad chances. Especially as he was setting up regular repeat gardening and lawn cutting.

You can leave flyer with shops and offices, in fact anywhere that people congregate. I know that most are thrown away, but it is a successful marketing tool compared to some other avenues. It takes about 5 leaflet drops before people usually notice them unless you have a product or service that they want right now. So, don't be impatient. I'd suggest dropping to the same homes every 3 or 4 weeks. You will see results gradually happen. Sometimes people file a leaflet in case they need the service in the future, and I've had enquiries up to 18 months after.

You could also use A6, which is postcard size because people will pin those up on a noticeboard they have in their home or somewhere convenient.

Your leaflets must have your business name, clear description of the product of service, website, e-mail, mobile number and area (you need not put an address), but the location is good so people know you are local. Photographs are very good and good bright colour. They are best when there is not too much print. You can always use the reverse for full details.

You can include leaflets with invoices and any other correspondence you send out. Do a share and get other businesses that don't compete with you to take some leaflets to distribute and do the same for them.

If you are delivering or carrying out work at a property, then leave leaflets at adjoining properties. If you have 20 minutes, then leaflet the whole road.

PRESS RELEASES

Local newspapers and TV stations are always looking for interesting stories and the reporters are busy so if they see a well written press release with a photograph or two, then they will be more inclined to use the story.

Press Releases need a title, something catchy, centred and in bold, and your name .It should be short and to the point. You need to be word perfect, get a friend to check it out and use spell-check.

The first paragraph should sum up the story. The next paragraphs should elaborate it. Try to include a quotation Mr Smith said "blah blah blah" and be precise.

Write "End" on a separate line.

Then put your name, e-mail, website detail,

mobile number and Business name and website.
Try to include some interesting photos.

I used to write a press release every month, finding a new angle. And I built up a relationship with my local reporter (they usually cover a specific area for general news), and we met up for a coffee now and again. I'd also call if I heard any real news and tell them to put me in good stead.

Press releases can be sent to national newspapers, magazines and TV stations. You may be surprised with the outcome.

WRITING ARTICLES

Local newspapers and magazines are always looking for interesting stories and regular contributors. Let's say you were offering a gardening service then write a regular gardening column. It doesn't need to be long. Make sure your details are published at the bottom and ask the editor for a free advert. If you don't ask you won't get.

Regular articles will make you stand out and readers will remember you. This does take some effort, but it should bring in extra business I the long run.

NETWORKING

Networking means meeting up with other businesspeople and sharing information about possible new customers. You can network by meeting another business-person over a coffee or you can attend specific networking meetings. The main thing is to share, be generous and you will reap benefits.

There are networking groups, the most known one being BNI who are worldwide. They hold local meetings and members are business-people from different areas. It is usual to only have one from each trade or profession, so you might have one electrician, one solicitor etc. They usually meet early, 7am and have a breakfast. Meeting once a week they can be penalized for missing meetings but can send a substitute along to represent them. The substitute can talk about their own business. There is a general chat then they assemble around a large dining table for breakfast. After eating and chatting to the adjoining members, they start, and each gives a one-minute presentation about their business and the types of customers they seek. Then they each say if they have any referrals for other members or testimonials. Each should have at least one referral. They also say how much business they have generated from leads they have been given. Finally, a member will give a longer presentation at each meeting, so others are more familiar with their business. Business cards for each member are stored in a box which is circulated so others can take out any card they feel they might find useful. In the UK it was £500 a year paid upfront and the cost of the breakfast, about £10 each time. Members must attend every weekly meeting or send a substitute (who can talk about their business). If a member misses 3 meetings they are suspended. This is not cheap, and it depends on your business. Some are more suitable than others. If you join, then have reasonable expectations and consider your investment. But test the water first by finding an existing member and ask to by their guest.

There are other business networking groups such as The Federation of Small Businesses which offer other services, 4Networking and the Chambers of Commerce.

You might find local government free networking meetings. Just ask around.

You should give out business cards to everyone (you can never know who might buy from you or know someone who is looking for your offer). Business cards are dirt cheap and should include a one-line description of your products or services (called the tagline). I once picked up a good order when I spoke to someone in a lift and gave them a card.

Start your own networking. Meet up with other businesspeople in different, no competitive fields, and share information. Have a coffee together and an informal chat. This will give you an idea if you like and trust them before you suggest anything. And if you find someone and you do all the giving with nothing back, then stop.

If there are exhibitions, like trade shows, business shows etc. then go along and talk to the exhibitors. Leave them cards too, but you must also show interest in their business. Don't dash in and push yourself. You are there free; they have paid for their stand.

TALKS AND SEMINARS

I've talked at many seminars successfully. Most people are afraid of public speaking but if you want business you must do some things you fear. And you will overcome your fear fast.

Write a script and learn it, rehearse in front of a mirror, then family and friends. You will get confident. Then when the big day comes you will naturally feel stressed when you stand up but concentrate on individuals as you speak, and the fear will drain away. You may not remember what you said but you will be surprised how confident you sounded. You might make mistakes but in most cases nobody will notice. Public speaking is a great way to get noticed.

WEBINARS AND YOUTUBE CHANNELS.
You can make videos from your home, your bedroom, out in the park. Anywhere. You can use your mobile phone. Keep videos short and pertinent.

A YouTube channel will build up followers who are interested in what you do. And from that you can gain customers. Do not make your channel a sales channel because that will turn viewers off. Make videos about pertinent happenings around your business, products or services, but also add some personal points, like a comment about the weather, what you have planned for the weekend etc. For example, a plumber might give handy hints on what can be done at home. You'll not lose business because viewers will be worldwide. Local viewers who like what you do will begin to like and trust you and ultimately, they will use you when they have a need. Put your details at the end of the video and in the description below. Spend some time looking at what competitors are doing online.

There are many people who are making a good living on YouTube, but it takes planning and knowledge to be successful. There is too much to set that out in this book. Do not be deterred but find the "know-how" on YouTube, the best learning platform.

Complete the information page for each video including tags, and your website. And have a good thumbnail image. You can make these yourself on sites such as www.canva.com for free. Be consistent.

Webinars are good ways to sell digital products such as courses and software. They describe problems and give the solution. You can give good information away in a webinar as this builds up confidence. You can prepare a slide show and do a voice over if you do not have confidence but being on screen yourself will strengthen your brand. Watch a few and you can trial a couple before you get serious.

Zoom and similar platforms allow you to have live seminars/webinars/meetings and see all the participants. These have become the norm since the Pandemic.

Free Gifts.
Everybody loves a free gift. The door-to-door brush salesmen used to give a free gift to anybody

who listened to them. They had tiny sample polish tins, funnels, clothes repair kits, needle threaders and much more.

Depending on your product price and sales you can plan your free gift. There are wide extremes. If you are offering a repeat service or product to a small number of customer's, you can pay more for your gifts. If it's a low value item, you'll pick something like car key rings which are cheap as chips. The main requirement is that your details are on the product. Tagline, website and phone number. These can be giveaways when you are looking for business, to new customers who you want to return or to regular customers. Great to give away at exhibitions.

Newsletters

These can be e-mail newsletters or hard printed copies depending again on the number of customers, where they buy your product and their location. For example, if you have an internet business then it makes sense to distribute through e-mail: on the other hand, if your customers buy from local shops then you might leave free copies at the retailers.

Your newsletter should not be a giant advert but contain information that will draw the reader in and interest them. A friend started with a very short enewsletter on street photography. He had a great deal of interest and it brought customers for his photographic business. He developed this and now produces a printed monthly newsletter that retails at $18, containing many useful tips and ideas but also promotes his business. After just 6 months he is printing 500 copies a month and growing. So not only is he promoting his business, but he has discovered a new profitable revenue stream.

You might even include other products, maybe a review, and get the supplier to pay you for that. This is quite legitimate provided you note somewhere on the newsletter that you might be rewarded for showing the product!

OTHER MARKETING IDEAS

There are hundreds of other marketing ideas that you can use, many involve expense such as advertising or hiring a marketing guru. You might wish to use those ideas and some support as you grown but I highly suggest that you use the many ideas, some really simple and most pretty obvious, in this book at you will not have to pay out much. Shoestring marketing such as in this book produces high impact and low-cost ideas that work.

I do hope you have found this a useful manual and that you will try as many ideas as possible.

Some might not work for you, abandon these and maybe consider them later.

Good luck in your endeavor to be successful. We can all achieve those dreams if we apply ourselves. It is just one step at a time.

COMPREHENSIVE MARKETING TICK LIST

Complete to find strengths, weaknesses and ways to improve. Take your time and complete this questionnaire, filling out details on the right side. This will become a useful reference that you can refer to and see how you are doing. You might wish to photocopy these sheets onto A4 pages to give you more room. The Central column is a simple Yes or No. The right hand column is for notes

Name of Business		
Contact name		
Position		
Address		
Landline		
Mobile		
Website(s)		
Blog		

SALES & MARKETING SUCCESS BLUEPRINT

Is this a Life-style business where you just want to make a living?		
If so, have you considered replacement capital equipment, pension, sickness, what will happen when you retire, can't do the work		
Is this a growing business where you want to employ other people?		
How many staff are there today?		
Do you delegate to a Manager?		
Where do you see the business in 5 years		
What is your eventual aim with the business?		
Do you have an active Marketing Plan? How often do you refer and update it?		

Have you carried out a market survey on the product? What did you find?		
Have you carried out a market survey on the price? What did you find?		
Who are your prospects? What are your market segments? Describe them		

SALES & MARKETING SUCCESS BLUEPRINT

Have you carried out a survey of your targeted prospects? If so, what did you do?		
If so, were you surprised at any issues they raised or their list of reasons for wanting your products and your Company? What were they?		
Have you carried out a SWOT		

SALES & MARKETING SUCCESS BLUEPRINT

Strengths		
Weaknesses		
Opportunities		
Threats		
What percentage of total turnover is marketing budget?		
Do you monitor this?		

SALES & MARKETING SUCCESS BLUEPRINT

Are you developing new products? If so, what direction are you going? The same type or diversifying		
Look at your existing marketing.		
Do you use radio or TV advertising?		
Yellow Pages, Thompson's Directories etc		
Direct mail. If so what		
If so, is it targeted		
Do you test?		
Telephone canvassing		
Is there a script		
Private Exhibitions		
Exhibitor at general exhibitions		
Newspapers		
Magazines		
Cinema		
Leaflets at Point of Sale		

SALES & MARKETING SUCCESS BLUEPRINT

Door to door leaflets		
Brochures		
DVD/cd or other multi-media		
Road running or stationery Advertising Trailers		
Web Directories		
Street banners or posters?		
Do you give talks		
Any other advertising?		
Do you log all new enquiries and see note where they came from?		
Are all leads followed up same day and then prioritised		
Are all leads pursued with a follow-up plan? (What is your average to get sale)		
When do you stop following up?		
Do you analyse all leads that succeed to see any pattern in getting the order?		
Do you analyse all leads that fail by asking questions?		

SALES & MARKETING SUCCESS BLUEPRINT

When they are on brink of failing do you make any special offer?	
Do you check what works and what doesn't?	
Do you use Groupon or any other discount scheme?	
Sales Skills	
Have you or your sales team had sales training? If so what?	
Do you have regular targets?	
Do you keep a Sales Target diary? (ratio of canvassing, presentations, sales)	
Do you have regular Sales Meetings? (end of month, for example)	
If you have premises is the signage outside acceptable for name, type of business, tel, website	
If you use vehicles are they sign-written on sides and rear?	
Do you have a uniform?	
If so does it display logo or name?	
Do you have business cards? If so do they display?	

SALES & MARKETING SUCCESS BLUEPRINT

Company name		
Phone number		
Website		
e-mail		
By-line or description of business?		
Does your card display Facebook or Twitter		
Is the reverse side used?		
What for?		
Do you have compliments slips? If so, do they display?		
Company name		
Phone number		
Website		
E-mail		
By-line or description of business?		
Does it include Facebook and Twitter		
Is the reverse side used?		

SALES & MARKETING SUCCESS BLUEPRINT

What for?		
Do you answer the phone in person, not answer machine?		
If so, within how many rings?		
What is the greeting?		
Do you have your own receptionist or use a call centre?		
Do you call in a check the phone is being answered, as you want?		
If you use an answer machine does it have your voice or a digital voice?		
Is the message inviting?		
How fast do you get back to callers?		
Do you use e-mail?		
Do you keep a list of e-mail addresses?		
Is the list kept up-to-date and clean?		
If you don't have the answer do you respond anyway with a re-assurance message?		
Do you follow e-mail etiquette?		
Do you have a website?		

SALES & MARKETING SUCCESS BLUEPRINT

Do all pages and links work?		
Is the site up to date?		
Is it easy to find contact details?		
Does it show Facebook and Twitter		
Is there a newsletter?		
Is there a podcast/blog?		
Are there free items?		
Are there useful links?		
Is it possible to buy on the site?		
Do you deliver direct from site?		
Do you Use Facebook Business Page?		
Facebook Events?		
Update Facebook regularly?		
Do you use Twitter?		
Do you use # on Twitter to reach bigger market?		
Do you include photos on Twitter and is it linked to other Social Media?		

SALES & MARKETING SUCCESS BLUEPRINT

Do you use YouTube?		
Do you use other moving media for video or Slide Presentations		
Do you use YouTube to educate or actively promote?		
Do you import YouTube to your website?		
Do you use any other Social Media?		
Do your look for stories and write regular press releases?		
Are press releases professional and include photo?		
Do you have a stock of good photos suitable for press (action focussed)		
Have you developed local reporter contacts?		
Do you use text messaging?		
If so for what?		
Do you network? How do you do this? How many leads do you get a month? Quarter?		
Do you undertake any seminars or talks		

SALES & MARKETING SUCCESS BLUEPRINT

Do you use referral schemes? And if so what?		
What reward to you gives referrers?		
Do you have any exchange referral systems with non-competitive businesses		
Any other?		
And another		
Do you run promotions for new customers?		
What do you do to get additional business from existing customers?		
Do you run promotions for existing customers?		
What promotions do you run for new customers?		

SALES & MARKETING SUCCESS BLUEPRINT

Any other marketing activity		

CONGRATULATIONS

You have successfully completed the analysis? Did you find many areas to improve? That is natural. You now want to plan what you are going to do and how.

TAKE ACTION!

It is no good reading this book and thinking "Yes! There are some great ideas" and then putting it to one side. Excuses are easy. "I'll start next week", I don't have time right now", I've tried many of these ideas and they don't work for me" and so on.

You need to take action today, right now. Make some short notes and act within the next 24 hours and plan to put some time aside every day to work on your business rather than working in your business. That is the only way to success.

SO GOOD LUCK!

I do Skype 30-minute consultations where you can talk about any aspect of your business apart from finance. With money you should have an accountant or someone with financial training, that can give you some sound practical advice. If you want a skype call then e-mail me at ask@mikeleahy.com and we can arrange it.

NOTES
Keep an Acton Plan. This space might be useful for keeping initial notes.

A companion book to Sales and Marketing Success Blueprint. This book is crammed with over a hundred ideas to start a business, each one tried and tested, many used by successful businesspeople to make their fortune. Available from your regular supplier or e-mail ask@mikeleahy.com